James Dunbar

The Practical Papermaker

A Complete Guide to the Manufacture of Paper

James Dunbar

The Practical Papermaker
A Complete Guide to the Manufacture of Paper

ISBN/EAN: 9783337399016

Printed in Europe, USA, Canada, Australia, Japan

Cover: Foto ©Lupo / pixelio.de

More available books at **www.hansebooks.com**

James Dunbar

The Practical Papermaker
A Complete Guide to the Manufacture of Paper

ISBN/EAN: 9783337399016

Printed in Europe, USA, Canada, Australia, Japan

Cover: Foto ©Lupo / pixelio.de

More available books at **www.hansebooks.com**

THE

PRACTICAL PAPERMAKER:

A Complete Guide

TO THE

MANUFACTURE OF PAPER.

SECOND EDITION.

By JAMES DUNBAR.

LEITH: REID & SON, 35 SHORE.
LONDON: E. & F. N. SPON, 16 CHARING CROSS.
NEW YORK: E. & F. N. SPON, 446 BROOME STREET,

MDCCCLXXXI.

PREFACE.

In adding another to the many books on Paper-making which already exist, it is my aim to supply a deficiency in these publications which has long been felt by those engaged in the trade, and more especially by the workmen.

I have endeavoured, in the execution of this task, to convey some useful information on the manu-facture of paper, derived from an experience, both in home and continental mills, of twenty years; and what measure of success I have attained, I leave to my readers to judge.

Some of the suggestions I have made may not be found suitable in all mills; but of this I am certain, that there is not one maker who will not find some hint to an improvement on his present mode of working.

INDEX.

THE PRACTICAL PAPERMAKER.

Selection and Assortment of Rags.

THE selection and assortment of the raw material form a very important branch of the Paper Trade.

Rags are brought to the mill in an unsorted condition, and are called Mixed Rags.

The system of assorting and classifying rags in common use in this country, and the distinguishing mark given to each sort, cause considerable confusion to the tyro in the trade, and rather retard than facilitate the work of this department, which ought to be conducted on principles readily comprehended and easily impressed upon the memory.

The superiority of the system in vogue on the Continent—its greater simplicity, and therefore efficacy, and the great saving of time (a most important item in the economical working of a factory) effected by it—will be shown in the following description.

The Rag department in Continental mills consists of a two-storey building, on the ground floor of which all the cutting and sorting is done. The upper storey is fitted up with twenty stalls or compartments, numbered from 1 to 20. The rags, having been cut and overhauled, are hoisted to the second flat, and there deposited, under the superintendence of the foreman, according to their respective qualities in the numbered compartments, and thence taken to the willows in quantities of the various sorts, to make up the desired stuffs ordered by the manager.

The rags are known by number as follows :—

No. 1 Rags—White linen without seams, fine clean,
,, 2 ,,   White linen with seams, fine clean,
,, 3 ,,   White linen with seams, second quality,
,, 4 ,,   White linen with seams, third quality,

The three last-mentioned qualities are easily distinguished, for as the quality deteriorates the rags become thicker, and, the thicker the rags, the greater the quantity of sheive they contain.

No. 5 Rags—Blue linen without seams, first quality,
,, 6 ,,   Blue linen with seams, second quality,
,, 7 ,,   Blue linen with seams, third quality,
,, 8 ,,   Good linen, seconds,
,, 9 ,,   Coarse linen, seconds,
,, 10 ,,   White cotton, fine, first quality,
,, 11 ,,   White cotton, second quality,
,, 12 ,,   Coloured cotton, third quality,
,, 13 ,,   Sailcloth without seams, first quality,
,, 14 ,,   Sailcloth with seams, second quality,
,, 15 ,,   Fine hemp bagging, good clean,
,, 16 ,,   Good hemp bagging,
,, 17 ,,   Hemp rope, fine clean,
,, 18 ,,   Hemp rope, good clean,
,, 19 ,,   Hemp rope, free from tar, third quality,
,, 20 ,,   Broke from all the above except the rope.

The simplicity and efficiency of sorting the different rags by this method of numbers are evident; the workpeople having only to know that the higher the number is, the coarser the quality of the rags becomes. No. 1 is the equivalent for S.P.F.F.F.

Blending or arranging the rags for the different stuffs suitable for the various qualities of paper to be made is a work of considerable difficulty, and requires the greatest care. For example, a paper of a certain quality is desired : the difficulty is to blend that proportion of cotton with linen rags which will produce a paper, tough, strong, well-sized, and possessing those elastic qualities which will permit it to be folded into any shape without showing signs of cracking, as is especially necessary in book papers.

The most convenient, and at the same time most efficacious, mode of procedure is to form the various rags into stuffs, such as No. 1 Stuff, No. 3 Stuff, No. 4 Stuff, No. 5 Stuff, and stuff specially prepared for tissue and copying papers, composed as follows:—

No. 1 STUFF.

No. 2 Rags,	.	.	1200 lb.
„ 5 „	.	.	2800 „
			4000 lb.

No. 3 STUFF.

No. 4 Rags,	.	.	400 lb.
6 „	.	.	1200 „
„ 8 „	.	.	2400 „
			4000 lb.

The above No. 1 and No. 3 Stuffs are for specially strong papers.

No. 4 STUFF.

No. 7 Rags,	. .	1600 lb.
„ 9 „	. .	2800 „
„ 20 Broke,	. .	400 „
		4800 lb.

If the broke accumulates, a larger proportion can be used in making coloured papers, otherwise the above quantity is sufficient. Rags Nos. 10, 11, and 12 are specially reserved for blending, for thick papers, or for printings of a high class. Nos. 13, 14, 15, and 16 supply the place of any of the numbers for which they are suited. No. 1 can be drawn upon in the event of a special paper being desired.

No. 5 STUFF.

No. 6 Rags,	. .	1600 lb.
„ 8 „	. .	2400 „
		4000 lb.

This No. 5 Stuff is principally used for mixing with the Rope Stuff for tissue and copying papers, in proportions which will be given in the receipts for thin papers.

ROPE STUFF.

No. 17 Ropes,	. .	2600 lb.
„ 18 „	. .	1200 „
„ 19 „	. .	200 „
		4000 lb.

It may be mentioned that the qualities of paper on the Continent are known by numbers, No. 1 being the highest quality of writings and printings. The different qualities of paper that can be made from the various stuffs are as follows :—

From No. 1 Stuff, extra superfine or No. 1 papers,
    ,, 3 ,,   superfine and fine papers,
    ,, 4 ,,   fines, fourths, and coloured papers,
    ,, 5 ,,   thin papers ; also used for mixing with the
                 rope stuff, for cigarette, copying, and
                 tissue papers.

Classification of Home and Foreign Rags

According to the Method generally adopted in this Country, with their Distinguishing Names.

Superfines, S.P.F.F.F., S.P.F.F., S.P.F., Dark Fines, Grey or Green Linen, New Pieces, Sailcloth, F.F., L.F.X., C.L.F.X., C.C.L.F.X., Fines, Seconds, Thirds, Cords both dark and light, Outshots, Prints, and the various qualities of Hemp and Jute Bagging.

Superfines	consist of	superfine new white shirt cuttings,
S.P.F.F.F.	,,	extra superfine white linen, first quality,
S.P.F.F.	,,	superfine white linen, second quality,
S.P.F.	,,	fine white linen, third quality,
Dark Fines	,,	fine white cotton rags, well adapted for blotting paper of a good quality,
Green Linen	,,	fine unbleached linen cuttings,
New Pieces	,,	fine bleached linen cuttings,
Sailcloth	,,	canvas (worn) and new cuttings,
F.F.	,,	coarse Russian linen rags, first quality,
L.F.X.	,,	coarse Russian linen rags, second quality,
C.L.F.X.	,,	coarse Russian linen rags, third quality,
C.C.L.F.X.	,,	coarse Russian linen rags, fourth quality,

'The last four sorts of rags are easily distinguished, as there is considerable difference in the quality and appearance, the rags being thicker and sheivier as the quality deteriorates.

Fines consist of fine white cottons,
Seconds   ,,   soiled white cottons,
Thirds   ,,   extra dirty cotton linings,
Light and Dark Cords consist of light and dark cottons (thick),
Outshots consist of good, strong, and sound rags,
Prints   ,,   cotton of various grades.

Home linen rags are often mixed with jute and cotton. When jute is present in linen, the colour is not so good when manufactured. The simplest method of discovering the presence of jute in linen is to wash a sample, and treat with diluted chlorine, when the jute will assume a red colour, and the linen bleach white. With cotton in linen, destroy the cotton with sulphuric acid, and only the linen will remain.

Methods of Rag Boiling.

Description of Boilers—Steam Pressure—Quantities of Lime, Soda Ash, Caustic Soda, and Time of Boiling.

Boiling the raw material is the most important part in the manufacture of paper. Any neglect in this department cannot be remedied after the material has left the boilers; hence the necessity for the exercise of the greatest care and most unremitting attention at all times.

The foreman ought to have a thorough knowledge of the nature of the raw material. It is not merely sufficient to know that the material is either cotton or linen, but it is absolutely necessary to know how to bring that material to the highest state of perfection without injury to its texture, and with a proper regard to the cost. Much, of course, depends upon the facilities for boiling, and the quality of the water, whether soft or hard. These things must be taken into consideration, and arrangements made accordingly.

All rags, even the finest cotton, contain sheive, which nothing but judicious boiling will remove. Badly boiled stuff also consumes too much chlorine, and makes a poorer-looking paper than when properly treated in this department. Great waste. of chemicals ensues when proper care is not exercised; and more especially is this the case with esparto, one lot boiling with two to three pounds less caustic soda to the cwt. than others. Again, there is considerable difference in boiling summer and winter esparto. The summer requires more boiling than the winter, and turns out better,—a fact attributable to the smaller amount of moisture contained in the former.

Those in charge here should be thoroughly acquainted with these facts, and should see that everything is in its proper place and in proper condition, and that there is no leakage at the boiler doors, steam joints, or valves. When everything is in good order, and strict attention paid to cleanliness, this department wears an aspect of serenity and comfort, never seen but where method is followed and care exercised.

Continental System of Boiling.

Rags on the Continent are boiled with lime and soda ash in a very satisfactory and economical manner, as follows :—

No. 1 STUFF.

Lime . . 216 lb. ⎫
Soda Ash*   114 ,, ⎬ for 4000 lb. rags,

boiled for 12 hours with 30 lb. steam pressure in a boiler revolving horizontally.

Nos. 3 AND 5 STUFFS.

Lime . . 324 lb. ⎫
Soda Ash*   152 ,, ⎬ for 4000 lb. rags,

boiled for 12 hours with 30 lb. steam pressure in a boiler revolving horizontally.

No. 4 STUFF.

Lime . . 378 lb. ⎫
Soda Ash*   190 ,, ⎬ for 4800 lb. rags,

boiled for 12 hours with 30 lb. steam pressure in a boiler revolving horizontally.

Boiling of Ropes for Tissue, Copying, and Cigarette Papers.

Lime . . 648 lb. ⎫
Soda Ash*   456 ,, ⎬ for 4000 lb. rope,

boiled for 24 hours with 30 lb. steam pressure in a boiler revolving horizontally.

---

* 48 per cen .

Preparation of Lime and Soda Ash.

Milk of Lime is prepared and strained in the following manner:—Construct a large wooden box of 15 ft. long, 5 ft. wide, and 4 ft. deep, divided into three compartments, with false bottoms, perforated with ½-inch holes to retain small stones and sand. In the first compartment the lime is slaked and reduced to a powder; it is then put over into the second compartment, and converted into Milk of Lime. In the partition between the second and third compartments there is a moveable sluice, allowing the milk to flow into the third division in quantities regulated by the man in charge. In the third compartment there is fitted a revolving drum, exactly the same as the ordinary drum washer of a half-stuff engine. The milk of lime flowing through the sluice is strained by the revolving drum, on the same principle as that by which the water is lifted from a breaking engine, and is discharged through a pipe direct into the rag boilers. If the lime requires extra straining, a fine wire strainer can be put over the mouth of the pipe leading to the boiler, and the lime passed through it. The several compartments are furnished with large waste pipes, which, with a liberal supply of water, carry off all impurities and what the drum has rejected. This system is a satisfactory and cleanly one.

Soda Ash.

The preparation of Soda Ash is conducted in very different ways. Some introduce it into the newly-slaked lime while the excessive heat lasts which is generated by the slaking; others, again, put the soda ash direct into the boiler. The latter should never be done on any pretext whatever. Nothing should be put into the boiler without straining. The best method is to dissolve the soda ash separately, and strain through a fine wire strainer into the boiler.

By adopting the above principles, the boiling department is kept orderly and clean,—a most important object in the manufacture of paper, than which no manufactured goods are more liable to damage from carelessness and dirty habits.

Boiling with Caustic Soda.

Boiling with lime alone is a much better and safer method than any other for fine-textured materials. The rags certainly turn out better, and it is therefore more economical.

The quantities of caustic soda for the cwt. of the various qualities of rags are as follows :—

S.P.F.F.F. is boiled with lime alone, then washed in the boiler, and again boiled with 2 per cent. of soda ash.
S.P.F.F. is boiled with 12 lb. of caustic soda* per cwt.

S.P.F.	,,	,, 14 ,,	,,	,,
Fines	,,	,, 7 ,,	,,	,,
Seconds	,,	,, 6 ,,	,,	,,
L.F.X.	,,	,, 20 ,,	,,	,,
C.L.F.X.	,,	,, 27 ,,	,,	,,
C.C.L.F.X.		,, 30 ,,	,,	,,
F.F.	,,	,, 15 ,,	,,	,,

all boiled with steam at a pressure of 20 to 25 lb. for

---

* 70 per cent.

10 hours in stationary boilers without vomit, and also in boilers revolving horizontally.

Boiling Esparto.

Great care and attention are required in boiling this material, as when esparto is insufficiently boiled, and a repetition of the operation found necessary, a great waste of soda is caused, and in the end the material does not turn out so satisfactorily.

When a consignment of esparto is received at the mill, the smallest quantity of caustic soda necessary to boil it properly should be at once ascertained, and that quantity continued throughout until the parcel is finished.

When the necessary precautions are taken to have everything in proper order and condition, the under-noted quantities of caustic soda will generally boil the various espartos in a satisfactory manner :—

Fine Spanish Esparto, boiled with 28 lb. caustic soda* per cwt.
Medium Spanish Esparto   ,,   24 ,,   ,,   ·   ,,
Fine Oran Esparto   ,,   30 ,,   ,,   ,,
Medium Oran Esparto   ,,   28 ,,   ,,   ,,
Fine Susa Esparto   ,,   28 ,,   ,,   ,,
Tripoli Esparto   ,,   32 ,,   ,,   ,,
Tunis Esparto   ,,   25 ,,   ,,   ,,

all boiled for 10 hours in stationary vomiting boilers with 10 lb. steam pressure, care being taken to see that the esparto is sufficiently boiled before the liquor is run off.

To acquire the very desirable knowledge of boiling raw materials, considerable time and close applica-

* 70 per cent,

tion must be given by the young papermaker, and a thorough acquaintance with all its details (none are of such small importance that they can be passed over, however insignificant they may appear) obtained before he leaves the department.

Receipts for High-class Papers.

In making papers of superior quality, considerable experience and skill are necessary in selecting and blending the material. The following receipts will produce papers, smooth, strong, tough, and possessing elasticity of feel and clearness of colour :—

EXTRA SUPERFINE CREAM.

FOR 300 LB. DRY PAPER.

S.P.F.F., ¼ ; Dark Fines, ¼ ;
Green Linen, ¼ ; New Pieces, ¼ ;
4 oz. ultramarine, marked B.B.A.C. ;
1½ gill cochineal ; 40 lb. pearl hardening.

SUPERFINE CREAM.

FOR 300 LB. DRY PAPER.

Dark Fines, ¼ ; S.P.F., ¼ ;
Superfines, ¼ ; Spanish Esparto, Fine, ¼ ;
6 oz. ultramarine, B.B.A.C. ;
1 gill cochineal ; 40 lb. pearl hardening ;
14 lb. dry starch.

FINE CREAMS.

FOR 300 LB. DRY PAPER.

Medium Spanish Esparto, ¼ ;
Fines, ¼ ; F.F., ½ ;
7 oz. ultramarine, marked B.B.R.V. ;
1½ gill cochineal.

EXTRA SUPERFINE COMMERCIAL POST,
ANIMAL SIZED.
FOR 300 LB. DRY PAPER.

S.P.F.F.F., ½ ; Dark Fines, ¼ ;
New Pieces, ¼ ;
3 gallons engine size ; 5 lb. pure alum ;
5 oz. ultramarine, B.B.A.C. ;
1 pint cochineal ; ¼ oz. carmine ;
40 lb. pearl hardening.

SUPERFINE COMMERCIAL POST, ANIMAL SIZED.
FOR 300 LB. DRY PAPER.

S.P.F.F., ½ ; Dark Fines, ¼ ; Supers, ¼ ;
3 gallons engine size ; 6 lb. pure alum ;
6 oz. ultramarine, B.B.A.C. ;
1½ gill cochineal ; 1 gill archil ;
14 lb. starch ; 40 lb. pearl hardening.

FINE CREAM COMMERCIAL POST, ANIMAL SIZED.
FOR 300 LB. DRY PAPER.

F.F. Russian Rags, ½ ; Seconds, ¼ ;
No. 2 Spanish Esparto, ¼ ;
6 oz. ultramarine, B.B.R.V. ; 1 gill magenta ;
6 gallons size ; 10 lb. alum.

FOURTH CREAMS.
FOR 300 LB. DRY PAPER.

Second Fines, ¼ ; F.F., ¼ ;
No. 2 Spanish Esparto, ½ ;
6 pails size ; 30 lb. alum ;
9 oz. ultramarine, B.B.R.V. ; 2 gills archil.

FOURTH CREAMS.
FOR 300 LB. DRY PAPER.

Fine Oran Esparto, ½ ;
Tunis Esparto, ¼ ; F.F. Rags, ¼ ;
9 oz. ultramarine, B.B.R.V. ;
2 gills magenta ; 4 lb. dry starch.

SUPERIOR QUALITY OF DRAWING CARTRIDGE.

NO COLOURING MATTER.

Cartridge, $\frac{1}{2}$; good Canvas, $\frac{1}{4}$; good Seconds, $\frac{1}{4}$;

EXTRA SUPERFINE POST PAPER.

FOR 300 LB. DRY PAPER.

Supers, $\frac{1}{4}$; Green Linen, $\frac{1}{4}$;
New Pieces, $\frac{1}{4}$; S.P.F.F.F., $\frac{1}{4}$;
3 oz. ultramarine, A.C. ; 2 oz. carmine.
(The above is the highest class of post paper made.)

EXTRA SUPERFINE BLUE, High Colour.

FOR 300 LB. DRY PAPER.

S.P.F., $\frac{1}{4}$; Dark Fines, $\frac{1}{4}$;
Fine Spanish Esparto, $\frac{1}{2}$;
$9\frac{1}{2}$ lb. ultramarine, B.B.R.V. ;
$\frac{1}{2}$ lb. magenta lake.

CARD PAPER, SUPERFINE, Animal Sized.

FOR 300 LB. DRY PAPER.

S.P.F., $\frac{1}{2}$; Fines, $\frac{1}{4}$; Seconds, $\frac{1}{4}$;
3 oz. ultramarine, B.B.A.C. ;
1 gill archil ; 30 lb. pearl hardening.

DRAWING CARTRIDGE, SUPERFINE, Animal Sized.

NO COLOURING MATTER, AND NO CLAY.

Cartridge, $\frac{1}{2}$; Sailcloth without seams, $\frac{1}{4}$; Seconds, $\frac{1}{4}$.
(This is a superior cartridge.)

DRAWING CARTRIDGE, SECOND QUALITY,

ANIMAL SIZED.

F.F., $\frac{1}{4}$; Thirds, $\frac{1}{4}$; No. 2 Spanish Esparto, $\frac{1}{2}$;
4 lb. starch ; 20 lb. pearl hardening.

SUPERFINE CREAM ENVELOPE PAPER,
ANIMAL SIZED.
FOR 300 LB. DRY PAPER.

S.P.F., ½ ; Seconds, ¼ ; New Pieces, ¼ ;
3 oz. ultramarine, B.B.A.C. ;
1½ pint cochineal ; 12 lb. starch.

SUPERFINE HIGH BLUE.
FOR 300 LB. DRY PAPER.

S.P.F., ¼ ; Medium Spanish Esparto, ½ ;
Scotch Fines, ¼ ;
12 lb. ultramarine, marked A ;
¾ lb. magenta lake.

FINE HIGH BLUE.
FOR 300 LB. DRY PAPER.

F.F., ½ ; Fine Oran Esparto, ½ ;
8 lb. ultramarine, marked B.B.R.V. ;
½ lb. magenta lake.

Washing and Breaking.

Considerable experience and great care are required
in reducing rags to half-stuff. If more attention
were given to the first stages in the manufacture of
paper, the subsequent duties of those in charge
would be less burdensome, and the particular class
of paper desired produced with comparatively little
trouble, and a very small percentage of retree.

The rags should be gradually introduced into an
engine, previously half filled with water. When
the desired quantity (which should never be too
thick and difficult to turn) is filled in, go on washing, and let down the roll just sufficient to open up

the rags and let the dirt escape, at the same time using the stirring stick right above the sand-trap, round the sides, and at the back fall of the engine. This prevents "lodgers," or pieces of rag not reduced to half-stuff, hanging about, which, if allowed to escape, would cause knots and grey specks in the paper. The rags must on no account be cut up or forced, but drawn out into fibre without having the smallest particle of rag unreduced to half-stuff; and this can only be accomplished by a liberal use of the stirring stick and the valve hook at the back fall of the engine. When the stuff is in condition for emptying into the drainers, the valve should be drawn with care, and deposited on the floor until the engine is empty.

The man in charge of this department should be made to understand that the quality of the paper depends greatly upon his knowledge of his business and the cleanliness of his surroundings.

Before replacing, the valve must be carefully washed, as the hole on the top is always full of dirt and sand, which, when the valve is carelessly drawn, escapes with the stuff. Next lift the sand-trap plate, and remove carefully all impurities, replace the plate, and fill up again. Much depends on the treatment of the stuff in this department whether the paper will possess the requisite strength, for if too quickly reduced to half-stuff the material is rendered weaker, and the washing is insufficiently done; while, if the stuff is properly drawn out into fibre and timed, its texture is not injured,—it is better washed, and produces a stronger paper.

Draining and Pressing.

When the stuff is emptied from the washing-engine into the drainers, it immediately commences to drain, and, when properly drained for removal, is subjected to pressure.

The best method of pressing or extracting the water from the stuff is by the extractor or centrifugal drainer, which dries the stuff sufficiently either for gasing or conveying to the potcher, as the case may be. This department ought to be kept scrupulously clean, and should be supplied with a box to contain any stuff that may accidentally drop on the floor and get dirty. All boxes or waggons connected with it ought to be periodically washed, and kept perfectly clean. The floor ought to be washed once a day, and everything kept in its proper place. All this is necessary, not only to ensure perfectly clean stuff, but also from a sanitary point of view, as the workman will find that, where a system of cleanliness and order is adopted, the department wears a healthier and more cheerful aspect than where dirt and disorder are the order of the day.

Gas Bleaching Half-Stuff.

Gas-bleaching half-stuff is seldom resorted to in this country, but is still carried on in Russia, and is almost indispensable for bleaching the coarse linen rags so plentiful in that country.

Half-stuff, to be satisfactorily gas-bleached, must contain a sufficient amount of moisture, else the outside only will be bleached, and that even an indifferent colour. On the other hand, if the stuff is too wet, the same results will follow. In order to ensure, therefore, a good uniform colour, great care must be taken to see that the stuff contains the proper amount of moisture, and no more. A generally effective method of testing the state of the stuff is to squeeze it between the hands, when, if the pressure causes no escape of water, yet still retains a damp appearance, it is in a proper condition for gas-bleaching.

The method of bleaching is as follows :—Put 1600 lb. of half-stuff, in the condition mentioned above, loosely into a stone chamber, and seal it in such a manner that it will be perfectly air-tight. Into the lead retort, connected with this chamber by leaden pipes, pour 3 pails of water and 66 lb. of common salt; stir thoroughly, add 65 lb. of manganese; stir again, and close the retort. Next charge a leaden vessel with 119 lb. of vitriol, and let the vitriol drop into the retort containing the water, salt, and manganese, through a bell-mouthed bent syphon, which admits the vitriol and at the same time prevents the escape of gas. (Three hours must be allowed for the vitriol to drop into the retort.) Then heat the retort with steam for seven hours, and allow two hours for the gas to escape up the mill chimney. For fine stuff, such as willowed rope, one hour extra must be allowed for the escape of the gas.

The quantities of manganese, salt, and vitriol used for the different stuffs previously mentioned are—

No. 1 STUFF.

FOR 1600 LB. HALF-STUFF.

50 lb. manganese ; 50 lb. salt ; 80 lb. vitriol.

No. 3 STUFF.

FOR 1600 LB. HALF-STUFF.

60 lb. manganese ; 60 lb. salt ; 100 lb. vitriol.

No. 4 STUFF.

FOR 1600 LB. HALF-STUFF.

65 lb. manganese ; 66 lb. salt ; 119 lb. vitriol.

ROPES, FOR COPYING PAPER, &c.

FOR 1400 LB. HALF-STUFF.

81 lb. manganese ; 91 lb. salt ; 124 lb. vitriol.

Potching of Half-Stuff previously Gas-Bleached.

No. 1 STUFF.

FOR 600 LB.

15 gallons chlorine at 4¼ degrees.

No. 3 STUFF.

FOR 600 LB.

20 gallons chlorine at 4¼ degrees.

No. 4 STUFF.

FOR 500 LB.

12 gallons chlorine at 5 degrees.

Potching Half-Stuff.

The quantities of half-stuff filled into the potching engine should at all times be as uniform as possible ; for if the quantity of stuff is changed and the bleach not varied in proportion, an irregularly-bleached stuff will be produced. When the engine is filled, wash for some time with a finer wire than is used on the breaker. When thoroughly washed, raise the washer and introduce the bleaching liquor · in sufficient quantities for the material to be bleached, care being taken not to exceed the quantity ordered by the manager, not only as a matter of economy in chlorine, but also on account of the injury the stuff would suffer.

In the case of vitriol being used, a small leaden vessel must be placed in such a position that the vitriol will drop into the engine at the rate of one pound of vitriol in twenty minutes. The vitriol should be diluted before using, taking care, in order to prevent excessive effervescence and a disagreeable smell, that the vitriol be added to the water, and not the water to the vitriol. When the bleaching process is finished, the stuff is emptied into stone chests, each capable of containing two engines of material. These chests are fitted with perforated zinc drainers—one in the extreme bottom, and another running up the back of the chest, and connected with the one in the bottom. The stuff is generally allowed to remain in the chests as long as time will permit, but, to ensure a regularly-coloured stuff, it is better to allow a fixed time.

Beating Engine Department.

This is another very important department in the paper mill, and should be roomy, and kept in good order, and perfectly clean. The man in charge should be a thoroughly-experienced workman, in whom every confidence can be placed, who will not add to or take from any order given by the manager without previous consultation.

The journals of the roll shaft should be frequently wiped, and no stuff should be allowed to escape at the ends of the roll or from below the edge of the roll cover, as the continual vibration of the cover rubs the stuff, and forms it into small black specks, which escape with it and show in the paper. In order to ensure a uniform colour, everything must be put into the engine in proper order, at the right time, and in the exact quantities ordered; nor should anything be put into the engine without being previously strained, no matter how clean it may be, as, by this system, straining, when actually required, is never neglected, for which there can be no excuse. Colouring matter should be measured or weighed, as the case may be, with the greatest exactness. Size and alum should also be carefully measured.

Whenever the engine is filled, commence washing, and continue for some time. In making animal-sized papers, a quantity of antichlorine should be introduced immediately the washing is finished, to neutralize the chlorine; but with engine-sized papers the loading should be first introduced, then the size, then the alum, and lastly the colouring matter. The water bags should never be shaken or squeezed, and, when they show any signs of being dirty, should be at once changed. The preparation of the stuff must be timed according to the thickness of the paper wanted, and, in proportion to the uniformity of time used in preparing a lot to be made at a given weight, will the regularity in quality and weight run at the machine.

Much depends on the workmen in this department whether the pulp is of the desired quality or not. A comparatively weak material can be made into a reasonably strong paper, if properly treated in the beating engine ; but if the stuff is carelessly handled, such as by sending out stuff for laid paper too fast and long, or too soft and carrying too much water, the weight will vary, and the paper crush at the couchers and stick at the press rolls, causing all sorts of trouble and confusion to the machineman, and a considerable amount of waste.

The following are some receipts for Coloured Papers. To ensure the desired shades, the colouring matters must be introduced exactly as stated, and at the intervals mentioned here.   .

COLOURED PAPERS.

DEEP LILAC.

FOR 250 LB. DRY PAPER.

No. 3 Stuff; 5 pails size ; 20 lb. alum ;
30 oz. violet methyl, marked B.B.B ;
½ oz. eosine, marked A.

DEEP GREEN.

FOR 250 LB. DRY PAPER.

No. 3 Stuff; 5 pails size ; 20 lb. alum ;
22 lb. silk green paste, extra fine.
(This is a beautiful clear green.)

DEEP LILAC.

FOR 250 LB. DRY PAPER.

No. 4 Stuff; 20 lb. alum ; 4 pails size ;
8 oz. diamond fuchine ; 3 oz. aniline blue ;
50 lb. straw pulp.

No. 10—P A L E G R E E N.

FOR 250 LB. DRY PAPER.

No. 4 Stuff, full bleached ; 4 pails size ; 20 lb. alum ;
¾ lb. bichromate, ten minutes later ;
2¼ lb. sugar of lead, ten minutes later ;
15 oz. Paris blue, dissolved in hot water, adding half
a gill of sulphuric acid.

No. 5—GREEN, MEDIUM DEEP SHADE.

FOR 250 LB. DRY PAPER.

No. 4 Stuff; 60 lb. mechanical wood pulp ; 5 pails size ;
20 lb. alum ; 2¼ lb. bichromate, fifteen minutes later ;
6 lb. sugar of lead, fifteen minutes later ; 1¼ lb. Paris blue.

No. 5—GREEN.

FOR 250 LB. DRY PAPER.

No. 4 Stuff; 60 lb. mechanical wood pulp ;
2½ lb. bichromate, 15 minutes later ;
6 lb. sugar of lead, fifteen minutes later ;
7 oz. Paris blue ; 4 pails size ; 15 lb. alum.

No. 12—P A L E G R E E N.

FOR 250 LB. DRY PAPER.

No. 4 Stuff, full bleached ; 60 lb. wood pulp ;
3 oz. bichromate ; 6 oz. sugar of lead ;
4 pails size ; 15 lb. alum ; 3 lb. Paris blue.

No. 3—GREEN, DEEP CLEAR TINT.

FOR 250 LB. DRY PAPER.

No. 3 Stuff; 1½ lb. bichromate ;
3 lb. sugar of lead, fifteen minutes later ;
2 lb. Paris blue, ten minutes later ;
5 pails size ; 20 lb. alum.

DEEP ORANGE.

FOR 250 LB. DRY PAPER.

No. 4 Stuff; 40 lb. wood pulp; 4 pails size;
20 lb. alum; 6 lb. bichromate; 18 lb. sugar of lead
25 lb. Venetian red; 50 lb. straw pulp.

No. 9—SKIN COLOUR.

FOR 250 LB. DRY PAPER.

No. 4 Stuff; 60 lb. wood pulp; 4 pails size;
20 lb. alum; 9¼ lb. green copperas;
10½ lb. crystal soda; 8 oz. bichromate;
1½ lb. sugar of lead.

DEEP OLIVE.

FOR 250 LB. DRY PAPER.

No. 4 Stuff; 60 lb. wood pulp; 4 pails size;
15 lb. alum; 2 lb. green copperas;
2 lb. crystal soda; 2¼ lb. Venetian red.

No. 6—BUFF.

FOR 250 LB. DRY PAPER.

No. 4 Stuff; 60 lb. yellow wood;
4 pails size; 20 lb. alum; 13 lb. yellow ochre;
10 oz. Venetian red; 1 gill Brazil wood dye.

NANKEEN TISSUE.

FOR 200 LB. DRY PAPER.

Nos. 17 and 18 Rope Stuffs, ¼; canvas, ¾;
3 lb. potash; 3 lb. green copperas;
2 lb. crystal soda.

LILAC TISSUE, Deep Shade.

FOR 200 LB. DRY PAPER.

Nos. 17 and 18 Rope Stuffs, ¼; No. 5 Stuff, ¼;
8 oz. aniline blue; 3 oz. diamond fuchine;
2 oz. violet methyl, R. R. R. R. brand.

WHITE TISSUE.
FOR 200 LB. DRY PAPER.
Nos. 17 and 18 Rope Stuffs, $\frac{1}{2}$; No. 5 Stuff, $\frac{1}{2}$;
5 oz. ultramarine, B.B.A.C.; 2 gills Brazil wood dye.

BLUE TISSUE.
FOR 200 LB. DRY PAPER.
Rope Stuff, $\frac{1}{2}$; good sailcloth, $\frac{1}{2}$;
2 lb. ultramarine, B.B.A.C.; 5 gills Brazil wood dye.

FINE GREY WRITINGS.
FOR 250 LB. DRY PAPER.
No. 4 Stuff, full bleached; 6 pails size;
25 lb. alum, 12 oz. bichromate, 2 lb. sugar of lead,
   to be dissolved together in one pail, and put into
   the engine while hot;
3 oz. Paris blue, half-an-hour later;
4 oz. logwood extract.

FINE GREY WRITINGS.
FOR 250 LB. DRY PAPER.
No. 4 Stuff, full bleached; 6 pails size;
25 lb. alum; 15 oz. bichromate; $2\frac{1}{2}$ lb. sugar of lead;
6 oz. Paris blue, half-an-hour later;
7 oz. logwood extract.

FINE GREY WRITINGS.
FOR 250 LB. DRY PAPER.
No. 4 Stuff, full bleached;
3 lb. ultramarine, B.B.R.V.; 2 lb. Venetian red;
4 lb. yellow ochre; 6 pails size; 20 lb. alum.

SUPERFINE GREY WRITINGS.
FOR 250 LB. DRY PAPER.
No. 3 Stuff, full bleached;
4 lb. ultramarine, B.B.A.C.; 1 lb. bichromate;
$1\frac{1}{2}$ lb. sugar of lead; 3 lb. Venetian red;
6 pails size; 25 lb. alum.

CATECHU BROWN WRAPPING.
FOR 250 LB. DRY PAPER.

Hemp bagging, ¼; No. 4 Stuff, ½;
7 pails catechu; 5 pails size; 15 lb. alum;
3 lb. bichromate.

CATECHU BROWN, DEEP COLOUR.
FOR 150 LB. DRY PAPER.

No. 4 Stuff, unbleached; 3 pails size; 10 lb. alum;
3 pails catechu; 2 lb. green copperas;
3 lb. bichromate.

ANILINE BLUE, DEEP SHADE.
FOR 250 LB. DRY PAPER.

No. 4 Stuff, full bleached; 5 pails size; 20 lb. alum;
4 oz. aniline blue; ⅛ oz. diamond fuchine.

No. 13—ANILINE BLUE.
FOR 250 LB. DRY PAPER.

No. 4 Stuff, full bleached; 5 pails size; 15 lb. alum;
3 oz. aniline blue; ¼ oz. diamond fuchine.

No. 70—ANILINE BLUE, DEEP COLOUR.
FOR 250 LB. DRY PAPER.

No. 4 Stuff, full bleached; 4 pails size;
15 lb. alum; 2 oz. aniline blue;
¼ oz. diamond fuchine; 6 oz. Berlin blue.

LILAC.
FOR 250 LB. DRY PAPER.

No. 4 Stuff, full bleached; 5 pails size; 20 lb. alum;
3 oz. aniline blue; ½ oz. diamond fuchine.

DEEP LILAC.
FOR 250 LB. DRY PAPER.

No. 4 Stuff, full bleached; 5 pails size; 20 lb. alum;
4 oz. aniline blue; 1 oz. diamond fuchine.

No. 4—DEEP ANILINE BLUE.
FOR 250 LB. DRY PAPER.

No. 3 Stuff, full bleached ; 6 pails size ; 20 lb. alum ;
4½ oz. aniline blue ; ¼ oz. diamond fuchine.

No. 7000—DEEP LILAC.
FOR 250 LB. DRY PAPER.

Nos. 3 and 4 Stuffs, half and half; 4 pails size ;
15 lb. alum ; 2 oz. aniline blue ;
2 oz. diamond fuchine ; 3½ oz. Paris blue.

No. 4—BERLIN BLUE.
FOR 250 LB. DRY PAPER.

No. 4 Stuff, half bleached ; 5 pails size ;
20 lb. alum ; ¼ oz. fuchine ; 5 lb. Paris blue.

DEEP ANILINE BLUE.
FOR 250 LB. DRY PAPER.

No. 4 Stuff, full bleached ; 5 pails size ;
20 lb. alum ; 9 lb. Paris blue ;
3½ oz. aniline blue ; 3 oz. diamond fuchine.
(The above blue presents a fine clear colour, very deep
and uniform.)

No. 8—VENETIAN RED.
FOR 250 LB. DRY PAPER.

No. 3 Stuff, unbleached ; 50 lb. chemical wood pulp ;
4 pails size ; 15 lb. alum ; 60 lb. Venetian red ;
3 pints Brazil wood dye.

FINE YELLOW PRINTINGS.
FOR 200 LB. DRY PAPER.

Spanish Esparto, ½ ; Oran Esparto, ¼ ;
2 lb. bichromate ; 4 lb. sugar of lead ;
3 pails size ; 10 lb. alum.

No. 70—DEEP VENETIAN RED.
FOR 200 LB. DRY PAPER.

No. 4 Stuff, unbleached ; 5 pails size ;
20 lb. alum ; 2½ lb. yellow ochre ;
50 lb. Venetian red ; 3 pints Brazil wood dye.

No. 58—PINK.
FOR 250 LB. DRY PAPER.

No. 4 Stuff ; 5 pails size ; 20 lb. alum ;
3 oz. diamond fuchine, dissolved in 300 ounces of
boiling water, and strained through a fine flannel
or silk bag.

DEEP EOSINE PINK.
FOR 250 LB. DRY PAPER.

No. 3 Stuff ; 5 pails size ; 20 lb. alum ;
12 oz. eosine, marked B.N., dissolved in boiling water,
and strained through a flannel bag into the engine.

PALE EOSINE PINK.
FOR 250 LB. DRY PAPER.

No. 3 Stuff ; 5 pails size ; 20 lb. alum ;
3 oz. eosine, marked B.N. ;
½ oz. violet methyl—strain into the engine.

EOSINE A—DEEP PINK TO BLOOD RED.
FOR 250 LB. DRY PAPER.

No. 3 Stuff, full bleached ;
13 oz. eosine, marked A ; ¼ oz. violet methyl.
  (This is a deep pink of a beautiful shade.)

YELLOW WRAPPING, FOR POST PAPER.
FOR 250 LB. DRY PAPER.

No. 4 Stuff ; 60 lb. mechanical wood pulp ;
2 lb. bichromate of potash, fifteen minutes later ;
4 lb. sugar of lead ; 20 lb. alum ; 4 pails size ;
50 lb. straw pulp, by Lahosse's system.

YELLOW PRINTINGS.
FOR 250 LB. DRY PAPER.

No. 4 Stuff, half bleached ;
50 lb. mechanical wood pulp ;
1¼ lb. bichromate, twenty minutes later ;
¾ lb. sugar of lead, half-an-hour later ;
15 lb. alum ; 3 pails size ; 50 lb. straw pulp.

No. 4—YELLOW.
FOR 250 LB. DRY PAPER.

No. 4 Stuff ; 4 lb. bichromate, twenty minutes later ;
8 lb. sugar of lead, half-an-hour later ;
20 lb. alum ; 6 pails size ; 40 lb. straw pulp.

No. 95—YELLOW.
FOR 250 LB. DRY PAPER.

No. 4 Stuff ; 20 lb. mechanical wood pulp ;
2¼ lb. bichromate, twenty minutes later ;
7¼ lb. sugar of lead, half-an-hour later ;
20 lb. alum ; 4 pails size.

No. 90—YELLOW.
FOR 250 LB. DRY PAPER.

No. 4 Stuff ; 40 lb. mechanical wood pulp ;
15 lb. alum ; 4 pails size ; 5 lb. bichromate ;
8 lb. sugar of lead.

No. 29—YELLOW.
FOR 250 LB. DRY PAPER.

No. 4 Stuff ; 15 lb. alum ; 4 pails size ;
1¼ lb. bichromate ; 5 lb. sugar of lead.

No. 23—YELLOW.
FOR 250 LB. DRY PAPER.

No. 4 Stuff ; 40 lb. mechanical wood pulp ;
15 lb. alum ; 4 pails size ; 5 lb. bichromate ;
11 lb. sugar of lead.

YELLOW PRINTINGS.
FOR 450 LB. DRY PAPER.

Tunis Esparto, $\frac{1}{4}$; No. 2 Spanish Esparto, $\frac{1}{2}$;
20 lb. French ochre ; 4 lb. dark English ochre ;
8 lb. sugar of lead ; $4\frac{1}{2}$ lb. bichromate ;
2 lb. red chrome.

YELLOW PRINTINGS.
FOR 400 LB. DRY PAPER.

Tunis Esparto, $\frac{1}{2}$; Oran Esparto, $\frac{1}{4}$;
$3\frac{1}{4}$ lb. bichromate ; 7 lb. sugar of lead.

CATECHU BROWN.
FOR 250 LB. DRY PAPER.

No. 4 Stuff, unbleached ; 4 pails size ;
20 lb. alum ; 12 pails catechu ;
6 lb. bichromate ; 3 lb. crystal soda.

CATECHU BROWN.
FOR 250 LB. DRY PAPER.

No. 4 Stuff, half bleached ; 4 pails size ;
4 pails catechu ; 20 lb. alum ; $1\frac{1}{4}$ lb. bichromate.

No. 134—CATECHU BROWN.
FOR 250 LB. DRY PAPER.

No. 4 Stuff, full bleached ; $4\frac{1}{2}$ lb. green copperas ;
4 pails size ; 3 pails catechu ; 20 lb. alum ;
$3\frac{1}{4}$ lb. bichromate.

No. 8—ORANGE.
FOR 200 LB. DRY PAPER.

No. 4 Stuff ; 50 lb. yellow mechanical wood pulp ;
20 lb. orange mineral ; $1\frac{1}{2}$ lb. Venetian red ;
4 pails size ; 20 lb. alum.

(The orange and the Venetian red must be carefully strained
through a fine wire or flannel bag.)

No. 68—ORANGE.

FOR 250 LB. DRY PAPER.

No. 4 Stuff ; 60 lb. mechanical wood pulp ;
15 lb. alum ; 4 pails size ; 30 lb. orange mineral.

No. 22—ORANGE.

FOR 250 LB. DRY PAPER.

No. 4 Stuff ; 60 lb. mechanical wood pulp ;
15 lb. alum ; 3 pails size ; 15 lb. orange mineral ;
1 lb. Venetian red.

No. 24—ORANGE.

FOR 250 LB. DRY PAPER.

No. 4 Stuff ; 50 lb. mechanical wood pulp ;
12 lb. orange mineral ; 15 lb. alum ; 4 pails size.

No. 95—ORANGE.

FOR 250 LB. DRY PAPER.

No. 4 Stuff, only half-bleached or gas-bleached,
and not potched ;
3 pails size ; 15 lb. alum ; 6 lb. bichromate ;
8 lb. sugar of lead ; 60 lb. superfine orange.

No. 70—VENETIAN RED.

FOR 250 LB. DRY PAPER.

No. 4 Stuff, half-bleached ; 2½ lb. yellow ochre ;
45 lb. Venetian red ; 20 lb. alum ; 5 pails size.

No. 125—ORANGE YELLOW.

FOR 250 LB. DRY PAPER.

No. 4 Stuff ; 40 lb. mechanical wood pulp ;
3 pails size ; 15 lb. alum ; 6 lb. bichromate ;
8 lb. sugar of lead ; 25 lb. Venetian red :
50 lb. straw pulp.

No. 2—YELLOW WRAPPING.

FOR 250 LB. DRY PAPER.

No. 4 Stuff, unbleached ;
50 lb. wood pulp, No. 2 quality ; 4 pails size ;
20 lb. alum ; 16½ lb. sugar of lead, brown ;
8 lb. bichromate ; 20 lb. Venetian red.

YELLOW OCHRE, FOR WRAPPING.

FOR 250 LB. DRY PAPER.

No. 4 Stuff, unbleached ;
60 lb. wood pulp, No. 2 quality ; 4 pails size ;
15 lb. alum ; 20 lb. yellow ochre ;
5 oz. Venetian red ; 4 oz. magenta lake.

PALE ORANGE.

FOR 250 LB. DRY PAPER.

No. 4 Stuff ; 40 lb. wood pulp ; 4 pails size ;
15 lb. alum ; 15 lb. superfine orange.

No. 115—GREY.

FOR 250 LB. DRY PAPER.

No. 4 Stuff, half-bleached ; 4 pails size ;
20 lb. alum ; 3 lb. green copperas ;
3 lb. crystal soda ; 4 lb. yellow ochre, dark ;
4 lb. yellow ochre, light ; 5 oz. Venetian red.

No. 34—VENETIAN RED.

FOR 250 LB. DRY PAPER.

No. 4 Stuff ; 40 lb. yellow wood pulp ;
4 pails size ; 15 lb. alum ; 48 lb. yellow ochre ;
50 lb. Venetian red.

(This is a beautiful deep Venetian red, principally used
for the covers of serials.)

No. 84—FAWN.
FOR 250 LB. DRY PAPER.
No. 4 Stuff; 4 pails size; 20 lb. alum;
2 lb. green copperas; 2 lb. crystal soda;
1½ lb. Venetian red.

No. 2—FAWN.
FOR 250 LB. DRY PAPER.
No. 4 Stuff; 20 lb. chemical wood pulp;
5 oz. ultramarine; 1 lb. Venetian red;
4 lb. yellow ochre, French.

No. 40—DEEP PARIS BLUE.
FOR 250 LB. DRY PAPER.
No. 4 Stuff, half bleached; 4 pails size;
20 lb. alum; 2 lb. logwood extract;
6 lb. Berlin or Paris blue; 2 pints cochineal.

SATURNINE RED.
FOR 250 LB. DRY PAPER.
No. 3 Stuff; 4 pails size; 20 lb. alum;
50 lb. saturnine red; 5 lb. superfine orange.

CHROME ORANGE.
FOR 300 LB. DRY PAPER.
No. 1 Stuff, full bleached; 25 lb. alum;
6 pails size; 56 lb. chrome orange paste, No. 1.
(This is a fine clear orange for a good quality of paper.)

SOLUBLE BROWN.
FOR 250 LB. DRY PAPER.
No. 4 Stuff, half bleached; 5 pails size;
20 lb. alum; 15 lb. soluble brawn.
(This colouring matter must be carefully strained into the
engine. It is the best substitute for catechu dyed
papers, and has all the characteristics of catechu, and
also the advantage of being much cheaper.)

D

VIOLET, Deep Shade.

for 250 lb. dry paper.

No. 3 Stuff, full bleached ; 25 lb. alum ;
5 pails size ; 6 lb. violet methyl, marked R.R.R.R.
3 oz. blue methyl.

COLOURED ESPARTO PAPERS.

DARK YELLOW.

for 400 lb. dry paper.

14 lb. bichromate of potash ;
1¾ lb. brown sugar of lead, dissolved in one pail
  of hot water—strain into the engine through a
  flannel bag ;
2½ lb. green copperas, one hour later ; 25 lb. alum.

ORANGE YELLOW.

for 400 lb. dry paper.

Oran Esparto ; 7½ lb. bichromate ;
15 lb. brown sugar of lead, dissolved in 5 pails of
  hot water—strain through a flannel bag ;
¼ lb. Venetian red ; 25 lb. alum ; 7 pails size.

FINE DEEP BLUE.

for 400 lb. dry paper.

Oran Esparto ; 1 lb. crystal soda ;
10 lb. prussiate of potash ;
3 lb. green copperas, dissolved in 4 pails of hot water ;
4 quarts iron liquor ;
1 oz. magenta, dissolved in one pail of hot water ;
25 lb. alum.

CHOCOLATE BROWN.
FOR 400 LB. DRY PAPER.

400 lb. Oran Esparto ; 37 lb. Venetian red ;
3 lb. catechu ; 5 lb. bluestone ; 5 lb. green copperas ;
4 lb. ultramarine—all one hour apart ;
20 lb. alum ; 7 pails size.

FINE ROSE TINT.
FOR 400 LB. DRY PAPER.

Medium Spanish Esparto, ½ ; good Oran Esparto, ½ ;
2 oz. eosine, marked A, dissolved in one pail of boiling
water, and strained through a flannel bag.

ROSE TINT.
FOR 400 LB. DRY PAPER.

400 lb. Oran Esparto ; 14 lb. Venetian red ;
1 lb. chrome yellow ; 20 lb. alum.

STRAW TINT.
FOR 400 LB. DRY PAPER.

400 lb. Oran Esparto ; 1¼ lb. bichromate of potash ;
3 lb. white sugar of lead, dissolved in one pail of hot
water ;
¼ lb. ultramarine ; 1½ pint iron liquor.

AMBER.
FOR 400 LB. DRY PAPER.

400 lb. Oran Esparto ;
¾ lb. chrome yellow, mixed in the engine one hour ;
1 pint iron liquor ; 20 lb. alum ; 6 pails size.

LIGHT BUFF.
FOR 400 LB. DRY PAPER.

400 lb. Oran Esparto ; 4 lb. green copperas ;
4 oz. sugar of lead ; 3 lb. bichromate of potash ;
15 lb. alum ; 5 pails size.

ORANGE BUFF.

FOR 400 LB. DRY PAPER.

400 lb. Oran Esparto ; 6 lb. bichromate of potash ;
8 lb. sugar of lead ; 14 lb. Venetian red ;
20 lb. alum ; 6 pails size.

FINE AMBER WRITINGS.

FOR 300 LB. DRY PAPER.

Medium Spanish Esparto, ½ ; F.F. Rags, ¼ ; Thirds, ¼ ;
6½ oz. nitrate of lead ; 3 oz. bichromate of potash ;
11 oz. Venetian red, strained through a silk bag ;
30 lb. alum ; 8 pails size.

PAPERMAKING MACHINE.

Great care is necessary for the satisfactory working of this department in the mill. Many changes occur to occupy the machineman : his attention, for example, would be immediately called to reduce or increase, as the case may be, the flow of water on the wire in emptying an extra fast or an extra soft stuff. To ensure satisfactory weight and uniform colour, two chests should be used, the beaterman emptying into the one, and the machineman working from the other. Every chest of stuff ought to be wrought separately, and, when made, should be ticketed No. 1, No. 2, and so on. By this means shading in the reams will be avoided, although a slight difference of shade should exist in the order, as it is at times unavoidable.

Paper machines in all mills are much alike, though

some of their parts (such as the sand-trap, which can be easily changed to the newest design at little expense) differ in every mill.

The best form of sand-trap is made in three compartments, through which the stuff flows 20 feet in one direction, and, turning, flows 20 feet in the opposite direction, then back again 20 feet, and falls into the strainers. This trap is covered with old wet felt, the pile against the run or flow of the stuff, and is hung at each end on pivots, and supported in an upright position by four legs upon hinges. When washing is required, lift the legs, turn the sand-trap round on the pivots, and wash out; adjust the trap again, and put the legs in position. This operation can be performed in from five to ten minutes. Pieces of lead 2 inches square should be in the bottom of the trap, and skimmers inserted about 2 inches into the pulp—the former to catch the heavy, and the latter to catch the light floating dirt.

The Wire.

There are many different opinions as to how wires should be worked, all, however, having the same end in view—namely, to run the wire as long as possible. A wire should never be tightened in a careless manner, or unknown to the foreman, whose duty it is to look after it.

It is certain that the slacker a wire can be worked, the longer it will last. It is, at the same time, a well-known fact that a tight wire runs steadiest, and gives the workman least trouble with crushing at the coucher rolls, and enables him to couch his paper hard, and causes less trouble in the frequent changing of the wet felts.

In changing, cut off the old wire, remove and carefully clean the tube and carrying rolls. Prove the rolls level and parallel—the bottom couch roll with the press roll, and the breast roll with the bottom couch roll. Put on the wire in the usual way, and place everything in position except the top couch roll. Turn the wire round by hand, and examine it carefully for blemishes; if any, make a note of them, and measure their distance from the seam, in order to know their exact position, and watch them, that the merits of a wire may be judged on a future occasion. Next put on the top coucher, and let the straining roll down with only its own weight on the wire. Prove the couch roll parallel with the bottom one, and run the wire for about twenty minutes, or while the strainer is being furnished. Tighten the straining roll just sufficient to take off the slackness, but not to stretch or rack the meshes of the wire; start, and run for some time. If the paper crushes, ease the couch roll weights, and work as little water as possible consistent with the closing of the paper. In a short time everything will come right; and the longer it is worked, the better it will be. If the couch roll jackets have been changed, some trouble may be expected with the couching. The wires should last from nine to ten weeks, working night and day at an average speed of 85 feet per minute upon a 60-inch or 90-inch machine.

Making Edges on Paper.

In Continental mills there is a method of making edges on the paper as it passes along on the wire, which saves the machineman much trouble, and is very useful to him in many emergencies.

Procure a piece of $\frac{1}{4}$-inch composition pipe; close up one end, make a hole in the centre of the closed end with a darning needle, and connect the other end of the pipe to the nearest water-tap with a piece of rubber tube; fix the end with the hole in it upon the wire frame between the two vacuum boxes; bend the pipe, and direct the fine jet of water upon the edge of the paper in such a manner as to give the edge the appearance of being cut. With this jet the edges can be made either thick or thin, to suit circumstances. If the coucher jacket is a little bare at the ends, and the paper hanging and creasing at the edges as it leaves the wire, the extreme edges of the paper may be thickened by slightly bending the pipe until it is found convenient to change the jacket on the top roll.

First Press Rolls.

This is a part of the machine where a considerable amount of waste paper is made, and any mode of preventing it must be of advantage as well to the manufacturer as the machineman.

The author has tried a contrivance which effectually prevents the paper breaking at the press rolls;

and if it should break and run across the roll, by setting this it will go just as far as is desired. Cut a long strip from the edge of a wet felt, and draw out a single thread from it about two yards long; lead the end of the thread inside the press roll frame, then tie a knot upon it, and lead it in between the paper and the top press roll. It will travel round with the paper and over the top of the "doctor," making a slight impression on the paper. When the paper breaks at the edge, it will run across to this impression and no farther, but will keep running up the press roll in a straight line with it, leaving an edge exactly as if it had been cut, which will not break at the calenders. A small groove should be made on the back of the "doctor," to keep the thread in the desired line for the different widths of paper. The thread will last about a week without renewing.

This method is a perfectly successful one, the author having had it in constant use when making thin papers. It saves broken, and can be worked so near the edge that the impression is taken off at the cutter. The reason for recommending the thread from the felt in preference to worsted, is because it is harder twisted, and makes a neater impression.

Cleanliness and Order.

Machinemen and their assistants ought to have soap and towel allowed them. The strictest cleanliness, especially of the hands, should be enforced. A considerable quantity of paper is destroyed by handling with dirty hands. To obviate this, a piece of felt for lifting off the rolls of paper should always be kept convenient. The floor and the pit underneath the machine must be kept scrupulously clean. It is a very good plan to have the sides of the pit lined with thin boarding, kept about an inch from the sides, so that the oil which accumulates on the framing will run down the walls without coming into contact with the boarding. On the floor of the pit a sparred bottom should be placed, to allow any sand or dirt from the feet to drop through the spaces; this will prevent the broken getting dirtied. The false bottom should be lifted twice a week and cleaned out. In washing up, all the corners and out-of-the-way places should be carefully cleaned.

In order to save time, when a wire is to be changed, all the tools necessary for that purpose should be collected together before the machine is shut; everything, in fact, ought to be in its own place, and ready when wanted. Nut keys should never be allowed to be removed from the machine-house, as they might be wanted at the very time they are in use elsewhere.

Finishing Paper.

The appearance of paper when finished depends greatly on those in charge of this department. Paper, to take the eye, must be made up in a careful and tidy manner. Careless tying, or leaving one sheet or quire projecting beyond the rest in the ream, should not be tolerated, for the market value of the article depends in a great measure on the manner in which it is presented to the scrutiny of the buyer; and the reputation of the manufacturer is often injured by carelessly or loosely tied reams going into the consumer's hands. It should also be borne in mind that carelessly put-up goods do not improve in passing through the hands of railway officials.

Paper sent out in web should be tightly reeled, and kept even in the edges. In this condition it will have a finished appearance, and command a better market, for the printing and uniform cutting is thereby greatly facilitated.

This department, like the others, should be kept perfectly clean and orderly. Cleanliness and order cannot be too rigidly enforced throughout all the operations in a paper mill.

Details of the Preparation of the several sorts of Colouring Matter previously mentioned.

CATECHU.

Boil in an iron boiler 25 pails of water, then add 200 lb. of finely-powdered catechu gradually, and keep stirring. Boil until thoroughly dissolved, which will occupy from two and a half to three hours of brisk boiling. Put it into casks, and let it remain until cold. While the catechu is cooling, dissolve 12 lb. of bluestone; let it also remain until cold. When both are perfectly cold, add the bluestone to the catechu, and stir well.

Care must be taken not to add either in a hot state, as by doing so the colour will be injured.

BERLIN BLUE.

Dissolve 100 lb. of yellow prussiate of potash in one boiler; dissolve 100 lb. of green copperas in another boiler. When both are thoroughly dissolved, let them be put together in a boiler with a close-fitting cover; then dissolve 20 lb. of bichromate of potash, and add it to the prussiate and the copperas. Boil again, and keep stirring; then add 17 lb. of vitriol, stir thoroughly, and let it remain for two or three days. Prepare some casks in the interval for the reception of the solution, by boring holes in the staves—say 6 in number—one above the other, and 6 inches apart, beginning with the bottom one, which must be 2 feet from the extreme bottom. Into these holes fit long plugs, which can be easily removed. When the casks are ready, fill up with the prepared solution, and allow them to stand undisturbed until properly settled. Then run off the water by the holes in the staves, removing the plugs one by one—beginning with the top one—as the cask gets empty, until the blue makes its appearance, when the plugs should be replaced, and the casks filled up with water again and well stirred; this washing to be continued four or five times, as circumstances will permit. The oftener it is washed, the brighter the blue will be.

PERNAMBUCO DYE-WOOD.

Put into a boiler 20 pails of water, and bring it

to the boiling point; add 200 lb. of Pernambuco wood, and boil for eight hours. Put it into casks, and wash same as for Berlin blue, adding 8 lb. of the muriate of tin.

ANTICHLORINE: ITS MANUFACTURE.

Procure a large cask,—or, better, have one made without the bulge which ordinary casks have in the centre; raise it upon a stand 3 feet high; fit into it two frames or screens, which can be easily removed when desired; work across this frame a network of white cord or twine of sufficient strength to support a weight of 200 lbs., and have it sufficiently close to prevent the soda falling through the meshes. Upon each of these screens put 200 lb. of the ordinary crystal soda of commerce, then put on the lid or cover, and clay it round perfectly tight. Make two or three small air holes in the clay, or have an air-cock attached to the cover underneath the screens, and attached to the cask a pipe connected to a retort, into which put 9 lb. of sulphur. Start a fire below the retort, and, when the sulphur begins to melt, heat a piece of iron rod to a red heat, and insert it into the sulphur, which will commence to burn and send its fumes through this pipe into the cask, passing through the crystal soda, converting it into an antichlorine. When this 9 lb. of sulphur is all consumed, the operation must be repeated, using again 9 lb. of sulphur.

Proportions :—400 lb. of crystal soda and 18 lb. of sulphur.

Dissolve the antichlorine in the cask, and bottle

it off into carboys, and convey it to the beating engine department.

BLEACH TEST.

Mix $\frac{1}{4}$ oz. of starch into a paste with cold water, then add boiling water until it amounts to one pint, adding two drachms of iodide of potassium; when cold it is ready for use. Drop a few drops upon a handful of stuff: if any chlorine is present, it will immediately turn black; if none, it will remain unchanged.

COCHINEAL: ITS PREPARATION.

Put 3 lb. of cochineal flies into a carboy; pour in ammonia until they are thoroughly saturated; let it stand closely corked for ten days; but if they get dry during that time, add more ammonia, then at the end of ten days pour the contents of the carboy into a flannel bag. Put it into a vessel three parts filled with water, and let it remain for 24 hours; then strain and squeeze the bag until the colour is all extracted. 3 lb. of flies ought to make 6 gallons of colouring, to suit the papers previously mentioned.

ENGINE SIZE—FRENCH METHOD.

This size, if properly made, ought to be as white as milk, and should not alter the colour of the stuff in the slightest degree. Boil 13 pails of water in a copper-shelled boiler. Introduce 90 lbs. of crystal soda, keep boiling for half an hour, then add gradually 200 lbs. of finely-powdered rosin, and keep stirring; boil for two hours after all the rosin is added, then add 5 pails of cold water, and boil again for an hour and a half; then put it into stock-chests, and allow to remain for ten days, or longer if possible. The best method is to have a number of stock-chests, each capable of containing a week's size, using out of the one while you are filling up the others.

Cubic contents of small rosin boiler, 38,714 cubic inches.

PREPARATION OF SIZE FOR THE ENGINES.

Put into a large copper-shelled boiler, three-fourths filled with water, 20 pails of this prepared rosin. Raise the heat to 40°, and add 120 lbs. of potato flour, previously mixed with cold water, to the consistency of cream. Raise the heat up to 60°, then put in such a quantity of water so that there will be of rosin 4 lbs., starch 3½ lbs., and of soda 2 lbs., in every 4 pails of the prepared size. In all, the boiler will contain 144 pails of size.

Cubic contents of large-size mixer, 153,400 cubic inches = about 202 pails, the pail being 756 cubic inches.

TURPENTINE SIZE.
FOR AN ENGINE OF 300 LB. DRY PAPER.

1 lb. potash ; 6¾ lb. turpentine ; 6¾ lb. starch ; 6¾ lb. water. Boil slowly, and keep stirring for 2 hours ; it is then ready for the engine.

SOAP SIZE,
MADE AND USED IN THE INTERIOR OF RUSSIA.

200 lb. tallow ; 35 lb. potash, dissolved in 15 pails of water, adding 14 lbs. lime.

Melt the tallow first, then add the potash water, one pailful at a time, until the grease is completely killed. Keep continually stirring, and be careful not to allow the size to spill while stirring, as it is very likely to do so.

The best proportions are as follows :—

7 lb. tallow ; 2 lb. potash ; 1 lb. lime ; 6 gallons water.
Boil 6 hours. Use 2 gallons to the engine
of 250 lb. dry paper.

TUB-SIZING—PREPARATION OF THE GELATINE.

Steep the skins in stagnant water until putrefaction begins, seeing however that it does not proceed too far, as the colour of the size will in that case be injured. Immediately putrefaction ensues, remove the skins, wash, beat them thoroughly, and put them into clean water, strongly impregnated with sulphurous acid. This arrests the putrefaction and bleaches the skins. Fill into the boilers, raise the heat to 150° for the first draught of gelatine, adding 5° to the heat for every additional draught. Run off the size into stock-chests, into which put a sufficient quantity of alum to preserve it.

Care must also be taken not to over-heat the skins in the process of extracting the gelatine, as by doing so the colour of the size will be injured.

PREPARATION OF GELATINE FOR THE SIZING MACHINE.

Take 100 gallons of pure gelatine and 10 gallons of thick prepared rosin size, without the potato starch ; mix together, and add 80 lbs. of alum dissolved in 40 gallons of water ; stir all well together, and heat to the desired temperature, and strain through a fine wire into the sizing box.

ANILINE COLOURS.

It is very important to the papermaker to have some knowledge of Aniline Colours, as they enter largely into the production of tinted papers.

The best method of preparing them is to dissolve them in wooden tubs, as follows :—Weigh off the required quantities, put them into the tub, pour on boiling water, and stir well. The proper proportion is one part of colour to 100 parts of water, which ensures a perfectly dissolved colouring matter. The solution should be prepared at least 24 hours before using, which assists the decomposition of the colour. Aniline Colours should be carefully filtered through a fine flannel bag,—or, better, through a white silk bag, which ensures a perfectly clean colour, and prevents specks on the paper.

The following is a list of the Aniline Colours most suitable for dyeing paper pulp, detailing their effect when used alone or combined with other colouring agents.

RED LAKE.

A fluid fast in colour, which produces a beautiful pink for extra superfine, superfine, note, and tissue papers; also well adapted, in combination with the best brands of ultramarine, for producing that warm cream colour (of a bright and clear appearance) so much desired in high-class cream wove and laid post.

This colour holds a prominent position for its great strength and durability, combined with cheapness.

EOSINE

Is a comparatively new colour, much used by makers of tinted papers on the Continent. It produces the finest shades of pink down to a deep yellowish red, and, combined with sugar of lead, produces a bluish pink on tissue—a deep and clear colour approaching to blood red.

LAC À LA COCHENILLE

Is a colouring matter, distinguished for its fine shade, and, on account of its cheapness, is well adapted for red and pink papers of a medium quality, such as posters, wrapping, and blotting papers.

DIAMOND MAGENTA

Is used for producing common reds, toning up news, and, in combination with aniline blue, for producing aniline blue papers and aniline lilacs.

VIOLET METHYL

Produces the brightest violet shades, also brightens up white papers, and, in combination with Paris blue, makes that deep blue which is so attractive to the eye, owing to its bright and handsome appearance.

PARIS BLUE

Is a colouring matter which requires care and experience in preparing for the engine, for it is often

E

sold in an impure state. Papermakers ought to see to its purity before using, as it is often considerably adulterated with starch, farina, clay, and other foreign matters, which are added to make weight, and are of no use to the papermaker.

The best brands are No. 1 and No. 5; they are of great yielding power for light and dark blue tissues and for ordinary papers.

Paris blue is sometimes sold in paste : when sold in this form, it never contains more than 40 per cent. of colouring matter. It is also supplied in pieces, which are easily soluble in water, and is very suitable for deep blue papers. The brands No. 6 and No. 7 produce very dark shades of blue by adding violet methyl. When consistent with the paper to be produced, a little dilute sulphuric acid should be added to the pieces, as it assists their yielding power, and brightens the colour considerably.

METHYL BLUE

Is a very brilliant colour, not affected by chlorine. It is much used in white papers, and for making fine shades of blue; it also combines readily with magenta for the production of lilacs.

SILK GREEN

Is a chemically pure colouring matter, producing beautiful shades of green; it can be easily tinted by the use of Paris blue or chrome yellow.

METHYL GREEN.

Used for very fine shades of green of a bluish tinge: when used with methyl blue, it produces all the shades of peacock green, giving a most beautiful effect.

ULTRAMARINE.

Ultramarine is used most extensively by paper-makers, not only to brighten, but actually to colour paper stuff. In common papers, such as news and printings, this colour is added to increase the liveliness of the paper, and give it a good bright whiteness. Ultramarine, however, is used also in blue papers of medium quality, and, when carefully made and of the finest quality, can be used for the best papers.

The two faults which act against the use of ultramarine in papermaking are the grit or small particles of hard foreign substances, and the inability of the blue to stand the alum used in sizing. With these disadvantages removed, pure ultramarines might be used for fine papers. It is a very necessary thing for papermakers to examine their blues, and this can be done very simply.

Weigh about 50 grains of each sample of ultramarine, and mix each well with 100 grains of terra alba, and look at the mixtures side by side in a good light. The eye can get a good estimate of colour from this test; but, to make more certain, examine the samples over again, only letting the price of each sample guide the weight in grains to be tested, and proceed in the usual way. Thus, supposing four samples at 65s., 72s., 76s., and 80s. respectively are to be tested, proceed as follows :— Bring each sample to a level so far as price per cwt. is concerned. The 65s. sample being 15s. dearer than the 80s., more of it can be bought for 80s., so the test must be carried out accordingly. If 80s. equal 112 lbs., 65s. will give you 138 lbs. The sum in each case is—

65	:	80	: :	112	:	138
72	:	80	: :	112	:	124
76	:	80	: :	112	:	118

By mixing these relative proportions of ultramarine, each with 100 grains of terra alba, upon white paper, the eye will discern the best sample for the money. In the case of the 80s. blue, of course use 112 grains.

To test its alum-resisting properties, dissolve the same amount of each sample in water, and mix in this water about ½ lb. of pulp. When thoroughly mixed, and each lot of pulp is well and evenly coloured, add one glassful of the ordinary mill alum liquor, either from pure alum or aluminous cake, to each, losing no time over the operation. Stir each well and continually with a glass rod, and note the glasses carefully as to the length of time each sample keeps its colour.

The above tests are excellent ones, and practically a safeguard to any papermaker in buying ultramarines.

SCRAPS OF CHEMISTRY

Connected with the Manufacture of Paper.

In these days of progress it is absolutely necessary for the papermaker to have some knowledge of
chemistry. It solves for him many problems, and
points out the cause of many difficulties with which
he has to contend, and their various remedies.

ALUM.

The alum of commerce forms an important item
in the manufacture of paper. Impure alum should
at all times be rejected, especially if iron be present
in it. Considerable difficulty is experienced at times
by the papermaker in producing a uniform colour
throughout a given quantity of paper; variations
occur, which, if properly investigated, will in many
cases be found attributable to the alum. Alum in-
tended for the beating-engine should be perfectly
pure, and ought to be weighed with accuracy, and
dissolved in a known quantity of water. This ought
to be tested at frequent intervals as to its strength,
which ought to be kept as uniform as possible. A
good system of ensuring a uniform supply of alum
to the engine is to fix a tabular statement in a convenient situation, so that the beaterman can command a view of it at all times. For example: the
beaterman is ordered to put in a given quantity of
alum at 5°; by condensation of steam it only stands
4°: the table should acquaint him at a glance how
much additional alum he is to use. All he requires

to do is to test the alum for every engine he fur-
nishes, which occupies very little time, and repays
him a hundredfold in the saving of trouble in strik-
ing the colour. This will be best exemplified in the
manufacture of blue papers. The slightest variation
in the alum varies the colour; hence arises the
necessity of great care, in order to produce the desired shade.

When alum contains iron in any considerable
quantity, it should be rejected. The simplest method
of testing its purity in that respect is to dissolve
a small quantity in distilled water, and add by
degrees a few drops of pure carbonate of soda to
neutralize any free acid; next add a few drops
of a solution of yellow prussiate. If any iron be
present, it will assume a blue colour upon the addi-
tion of the yellow prussiate solution. The intensity of the blue will indicate the quantity of iron
present. Alum should be periodically tested in this
manner.

ALUMINOUS CAKES.

In many paper mills where low-classed printings
and news are made, aluminous cakes are used in-
stead of alum. Aluminous cakes are made from
china clay, which is treated with strong sulphuric
acid in suitable vessels. The acid has the effect of
rendering the alumina soluble by dispelling the
silicic acid and forming soluble sulphate of alumina.
Hence aluminous cakes are valued according to
their percentage of soluble alumina. The examina-

tion of aluminous cakes must be undertaken by a properly qualified analyst. A great fault in aluminous cakes is the presence of free acid, and sometimes dirt, in abundance. Both these deleterious agents should receive the careful attention of paper-makers.

BLEACHING POWDER.

This is a very important chemical, and one which enters largely into the cost of working a paper factory; hence the necessity of the manager being in a position to know whether the article with which his employer is supplied is of the proper quality or not, as its value to him depends entirely upon the amount of chlorine it contains.

To test bleaching powder as to the percentage of chlorine contained therein, proceed as follows :—

Take 100 grains of arsenious acid; dissolve them in four fluid ounces of hydrochloric acid, which possibly will require a little heat; the solution is then diluted with 6 ounces by measure of distilled water. The whole ought to measure exactly 10 ounces; consequently each ounce will contain 10 grains of arsenious acid.

Take 100 grains of bleaching powder from various parts of the sample to be tested; rub it in a mortar with a little water, then add as much water as will twice fill an ordinary graduated alkalimeter; allow the coarse grains to settle, then fill the alkalimeter, which is divided into 100 parts. Each part will contain half a grain of bleaching powder. Take one ounce of the arsenious solution, and add to it a little sulphate of indigo, sufficient to render it of a distinct blue colour; then into this pour slowly the bleaching liquor from the alkalimeter until the blue colour disappears, stirring continually during the operation. Note the number of graduations required to effect this change.

Every 10 grains of the arsenious acid is equal to 7·2 grains of chlorine; so the quantity of bleaching liquor taken to decolour the indigo will contain that amount of chlorine. Suppose it has required 48 graduations of the bleaching liquor to effect the change, this will be equal to 24 grains of bleaching powder: therefore 24 grains of bleaching powder will contain 7·2 of chlorine; and if 24 contain 7·2, 100 will contain 30. The sample will therefore contain 30 per cent. of chlorine.

EXAMINATION OF SODA AS TO ITS CAUSTICITY.

The value of soda to the papermaker depends upon the amount of caustic alkali which it contains. The admixed salts contained in soda consist of various sorts, and are of no value to the papermaker. As the proportion of these salts varies very much, it is necessary to examine the soda periodically, to ascertain the quantity of caustic alkali it contains.

This can be done very easily, and by a re-agent which is applicable to both caustic soda and soda ash. Caustic soda differs from soda ash in that its alkali (pure soda) is in a free and uncombined state, whilst the alkali of soda ash is united to an acid—carbonic acid. This acid, however, is but a weak body, and the test, which serves to ally with the caustic alkali in caustic soda, is of sufficient strength to perform a similar function in the case of soda ash, by expelling the carbonic acid in the form of a gas. To effect this thoroughly, it is necessary to boil the solution of soda ash during the entire operation, in order that the carbonic acid gas should not dissolve in the water or solution of soda ash.

One equivalent of soda, represented by the figure 31, is exactly neutralized by one equivalent of acid, 40. The absolutely correct system of preparing the test re-agent above alluded to would be too technical an operation except for a properly qualified analyst. The following test, however, can be simply prepared:—Add to half-a-gallon of distilled water about 3 or 4 ounces (fluid) of pure sulphuric acid, and allow the mixture to get cool. Fill a " Winchester quart " bottle with this test acid, keeping the stopper close, and putting the acid in a place where the temperature is even and not liable to rise above 60°. Next weigh out carefully 25 grains of pure anhydrous carbonate of soda, and dissolve them in about one half an evaporating basinful of distilled water. The basin can hold, say about 1 pint. Set this over a spirit lamp or Bunsen burner to boil, having a good long glass rod in the basin, and having also added 5 or 6 drops of litmus. Meanwhile fill an alkalimeter with your test acid. Mohr's alkalimeter and clip, fitted also with a float, are the best things to use, and can be had of any chemical-instrument maker. The alkalimeter will contain 1000 grains of the test acid. When the solution of pure soda is boiling, add the acid cautiously, for fear of the effervescence causing overflow and loss. Add gradually until the litmus shows signs of reddening. Allow the solution to boil briskly now, and add the acid drop by drop until the litmus is of a purple tint. Note now whether this purple tint is stable after boiling, and if so, dot down the number of grains on the alkalimeter corresponding with the float-line; then add one or two drops more acid until the soda solution turns a permanent red, and dot down this number also.

Now, supposing the test acid denotes 800 as the first figure, and 810 as the figure when the soda turned red: take the mean, 805. Then 25 grains of pure carbonate of soda are equivalent to 805 grains of acid liquor, and of course *vice versâ*. The following calculation will give the strength of the test liquor :—

Carb. Soda.		Pure Soda.		Carb. Soda.		Pure Soda.
53	:	31	: :	25	:	14·56

Therefore 805 grains of the test acid are equivalent to 14·56 of pure alkali. This experiment must be made three times to prove the accuracy of the test liquor, as everything depends upon the latter being perfectly true, seeing that it has to do duty in every future case of testing.

Having found the above correct, the " Winchester " is duly labelled, and 25 grains of each sample of soda ash are taken and boiled, and tested exactly in the same manner. Suppose a sample of 25 grains requires 705 grains of test acid, the following is the calculation :—

Test Acid.		Alkali.		Test Acid.		Alkali.
805	:	14·56	: :	705	:	12·75

then 12·75 × 4 = 51 % alkali (say).

This test is very accurate, provided the test acid is not too strong, and is added cautiously so as not to produce violent effervescence.

In examining caustic soda the above test acid is used, but the sample of caustic is dissolved in cold water, and then examined in the same way. It is, however, better to take a piece of caustic and weigh it at once, and not endeavour to obtain any exact weight. Caustic is so deliquescent, that before it is possible to weigh out any exact given weight, the soda would probably absorb a large amount of water from the air. Weigh a piece about the size of a filbert, and, when the result is obtained, the following calculation will give the exact percentage :—

Weight of sample	:	Amount of alikali absorbed	: 100 :	Percentage of alkali in sample.

RULES TO BE OBSERVED IN THE EXAMINATION OF SODA.

All the vessels and glasses must be scrupulously clean.

The water used must be distilled.

The operator must take great care to read correctly the volume of the test acid used. Nothing facilitates this so well as a Mohr's float.

The tincture or solution of litmus must be kept in a well-stoppered narrow-necked bottle, and frequently in a dark cupboard. No alkali must be added to it on any account, as it will corrupt the result. Should the solution decompose or turn brown, one drop of weak ammonia may be added, but it is better to make some fresh solution.

COLOURED TEST PAPERS.

The most efficient test papers are litmus and turmeric; they surpass liquid tests in delicacy and general application.

LITMUS TEST PAPER.

To prepare litmus paper, rub good litmus with a little hot water in a mortar, and pour the mixture into an evaporating basin; add water until the proportion is half-a-pint of water to one ounce of litmus; cover up so as to keep warm for an hour, after which the liquid must be filtered, and fresh hot water poured on the residue. This is to be boiled, covered up as before, and allowed to stand. The operation is to be repeated a second time, and, if much colour comes, a third time.

The first solution is to be kept separate from the second and third, which may be mixed together. The first solution will not require evaporation, but the others may be so far reduced in quantity, that when a piece of blotting or filtering paper is dipped into them and dried, they will impart to it a blue colour of sufficient intensity for use.

The paper is then to be dipped in the solution. The paper—blotting will suit very well—should always be unsized, of good colour, and moderate thickness, say from 15 to 20 lb. demy, and cut into pieces of a convenient size for dipping. Particular care should be taken to use paper as free as possible from earthy matter, and especially from carbonate of lime. Sized papers produce a finer tint on the surface, but are not so delicate as a test.

Pour the litmus solution into a plate, and draw the slips of paper through it in such a manner that the fluid will come in contact with both sides; allow it to drip, then hang them across two thread lines to dry.

The tint ought to be a distinct blue, and may be tested as to its delicacy by touching the paper with a very dilute acid, observing whether the red colour produced is vivid or not. It should, when dry, be tied up into bundles, and preserved from the air and light. A wide-necked glass-stoppered bottle is best suited for this purpose. Put in the test papers, and paste round the sides of the bottle a piece of dark paper to exclude the light, as both air and light tend to destroy the colour and efficacy of the test paper.

TURMERIC TEST PAPER.

This paper is prepared in a manner similar to litmus paper. A hot infusion of finely-crushed turmeric is to be made by boiling one ounce of turmeric in 12 ounces of water for half-an-hour; strain through a fine cloth or silk bag, and leave the fluid to settle for a few minutes. The liquid should be of such strength that paper dipped into it and then dried should be of a fine yellow colour. The paper should be of the same quality in every respect as for litmus paper. No particular care is necessary in drying, as with litmus paper; but both papers should be prepared where acid and alkaline fumes cannot come in contact with them, as they injure the colour of both.

USE OF THE TEST PAPERS.

In using the test papers with a fluid suspected to contain free acid or alkali, or to find if one of them predominates, all that is necessary is to moisten them with the liquid and observe the change. If the fluid be acid, the blue colour of the litmus paper will change immediately to red; if alkaline, the yellow colour of the turmeric paper will change to brown. The moistening may be effected by dipping a glass rod into the liquid to be tested, and then touching the test paper.

These tests must be made by daylight, if a minute estimate of the change is necessary, as artificial light will not enable you to note the delicacy of the action of acid or alkali when a small portion is present.

BLOTTING PAPER.

This is a paper which, to bring it to a high standard of perfection, requires a greater amount of care and experience in its manufacture than is generally supposed. Every one who uses the article knows that its value consists in its absorbing qualities; and that depends as much in the mode of preparation as in the material from which it is made.

In selecting materials for blotting of a high class, cotton rags of the weakest and tenderest description procurable should be chosen. Boil them with 4 lbs. of caustic soda to the cwt—that is, if you have no facilities for boiling them with lime alone.

When furnished in the breaking-engine, wash thoroughly before letting down the roll; when thoroughly washed, reduce them to half-stuff, and as soon as possible empty into the poacher, or convey to the poacher as the case may be, and bleach with great care. When up to the desired colour, empty into the drainer, and drain immediately. It may be mentioned that the breaker-plate ought to be sharp when starting to blottings.

The beater roll and plate should also be in good order, and the stuff beaten off smartly, not to exceed one hour and a half in the engine. For pink blottings furnish two thirds of white cottons and one third of turkey reds if they can be got; if not, dye with cochineal to the desired shade, empty down to the machine before starting, and see that the vacuum pumps are in good condition. Remove the weights from the couch roll, and, if there are lifting screws, raise the top couch roll a little. Now take the shake belt off, as the shake will not be required. Press light with the first press, and have the top roll of the second press covered with an ordinary jacket similar to a couch roll jacket. Dry hard, and pass through one calender with the weights off, and the roll as light as possible,—just enough to smooth slightly. In this way the author has made blotting which was considered a good article.

EXPERIMENT MADE WITH MECHANICAL WOOD PULP,

PRODUCED BY ONE OF VOLTER'S MACHINES.

One cubic sachen* of the wood of the aspen, which had been in the mill yard exposed to the sun for 12 weeks, weighing 9340 lbs., produced 5384 lbs. dry pulp fit for manufacturing into paper, and 70 lbs. waste unfit for paper.

---

* Russian measure = 1 cubic fathom.

www.ingramcontent.com/pod-product-compliance
Lightning Source LLC
Chambersburg PA
CBHW022153090426
42742CB00010B/1491